Welcome to our Restroom
Please Get Comfy!

DEDICATION

This book is dedicated to all the hilarious and humorous people out there who want to make their bathroom guests smile.

Your are my inspiration for producing books and I'm honored to be a part of keeping all your bathroom guests signin all in one place.

This journal notebook will help you record all the funny things that all your guests will write.

HOW TO USE THIS BOOK

The purpose of this book is to keep all of your guests sign in and comments all in one place. It will help keep you organized.

This Bathroom Guest Book Journal will allow you to entertain your guests while they visit your restroom and give them something funny to read.

Here are examples of the prompts for you to fill in and write about yourself in this book:

Name, Sign In
Visiting From
Date, Time, (Day & Year)
DURING YOUR VISIT DID YOU . . .

Play With Your Phone?
Mess With Your Hair?
Inspect Your Teeth For Food?
Check Your Butt In The Mirror?
Read Through This Entire Guest Book?
CHECK ALL THAT APPLY . . .

I Take Restroom Selfies
I Snoop In Medicine Cabinets
I Text/ Call While On The Toilet
I Pick My Nose In The Restroom
I Talk To Myself While On The Toilet

Welcome to our Restroom
Please Seat Yourself!

Name: _____
Visiting From: _____
Date: _____ Time: _____
Reason for Visit: _____

Your Favorite Name(s) for this Room?
- ☐ Powder Room
- ☐ Crapper
- ☐ John
- ☐ The office
- ☐ Can
- ☐ Other....

During Your Visit Did you...
- ☐ Play with your smartphone?
- ☐ Mess with your hair?
- ☐ Inspect your teeth for food?
- ☐ Check out your butt in the mirror?
- ☐ Check your zipper/fly?
- ☐ Read through this entire guest book?

Please Tick All That Apply
- ☐ I take restroom selfies
- ☐ I snoop in medicine cabinets
- ☐ I text/call while on the toilet
- ☐ I pick my nose in the restroom
- ☐ I talk to myself while on the toilet

Doodles & Brilliant Thoughts Inspired by the Throne

Welcome to our Restroom
Please Seat Yourself!

Name: _____
Visiting From: _____
Date: _____ Time: _____
Reason for Visit: _____

Your Favorite Name(s) for this Room?
- ☐ Powder Room
- ☐ The office
- ☐ Crapper
- ☐ Can
- ☐ John
- ☐ Other....

During Your Visit Did you...
- ☐ Play with your smartphone?
- ☐ Mess with your hair?
- ☐ Inspect your teeth for food?
- ☐ Check out your butt in the mirror?
- ☐ Check your zipper/fly?
- ☐ Read through this entire guest book?

Please Tick All That Apply
- ☐ I take restroom selfies
- ☐ I snoop in medicine cabinets
- ☐ I text/call while on the toilet
- ☐ I pick my nose in the restroom
- ☐ I talk to myself while on the toilet

Doodles & Brilliant Thoughts Inspired by the Throne

Welcome to our Restroom
Please Seat Yourself!

Name: _____
Visiting From: _____
Date: _____ Time: _____
Reason for Visit: _____

Your Favorite Name(s) for this Room?
- ☐ Powder Room
- ☐ Crapper
- ☐ John
- ☐ The office
- ☐ Can
- ☐ Other....

During Your Visit Did you...
- ☐ Play with your smartphone?
- ☐ Mess with your hair?
- ☐ Inspect your teeth for food?
- ☐ Check out your butt in the mirror?
- ☐ Check your zipper/fly?
- ☐ Read through this entire guest book?

Please Tick All That Apply
- ☐ I take restroom selfies
- ☐ I snoop in medicine cabinets
- ☐ I text/call while on the toilet
- ☐ I pick my nose in the restroom
- ☐ I talk to myself while on the toilet

Doodles & Brilliant Thoughts Inspired by the Throne

 # Welcome to our Restroom
Please Seat Yourself!

Name: ———————————
Visiting From: ———————————
Date: ——————— Time: ———————
Reason for Visit: ———————————

Your Favorite Name(s) for this Room?
- ☐ Powder Room
- ☐ Crapper
- ☐ John
- ☐ The office
- ☐ Can
- ☐ Other….

During Your Visit Did you…
- ☐ Play with your smartphone?
- ☐ Mess with your hair?
- ☐ Inspect your teeth for food?
- ☐ Check out your butt in the mirror?
- ☐ Check your zipper/fly?
- ☐ Read through this entire guest book?

Please Tick All That Apply
- ☐ I take restroom selfies
- ☐ I snoop in medicine cabinets
- ☐ I text/call while on the toilet
- ☐ I pick my nose in the restroom
- ☐ I talk to myself while on the toilet

Doodles & Brilliant Thoughts Inspired by the Throne

Welcome to our Restroom
Please Seat Yourself!

Name: _____
Visiting From: _____
Date: _____ Time: _____
Reason for Visit: _____

Your Favorite Name(s) for this Room?
- ☐ Powder Room
- ☐ Crapper
- ☐ John
- ☐ The office
- ☐ Can
- ☐ Other....

During Your Visit Did you...
- ☐ Play with your smartphone?
- ☐ Mess with your hair?
- ☐ Inspect your teeth for food?
- ☐ Check out your butt in the mirror?
- ☐ Check your zipper/fly?
- ☐ Read through this entire guest book?

Please Tick All That Apply
- ☐ I take restroom selfies
- ☐ I snoop in medicine cabinets
- ☐ I text/call while on the toilet
- ☐ I pick my nose in the restroom
- ☐ I talk to myself while on the toilet

Doodles & Brilliant Thoughts Inspired by the Throne

Welcome to our Restroom
Please Seat Yourself!

Name: _____
Visiting From: _____
Date: _____ Time: _____
Reason for Visit: _____

Your Favorite Name(s) for this Room?
- ☐ Powder Room
- ☐ The office
- ☐ Crapper
- ☐ Can
- ☐ John
- ☐ Other....

During Your Visit Did you...
- ☐ Play with your smartphone?
- ☐ Mess with your hair?
- ☐ Inspect your teeth for food?
- ☐ Check out your butt in the mirror?
- ☐ Check your zipper/fly?
- ☐ Read through this entire guest book?

Please Tick All That Apply
- ☐ I take restroom selfies
- ☐ I snoop in medicine cabinets
- ☐ I text/call while on the toilet
- ☐ I pick my nose in the restroom
- ☐ I talk to myself while on the toilet

Doodles & Brilliant Thoughts Inspired by the Throne

 # Welcome to our Restroom
Please Seat Yourself!

Name: _____
Visiting From: _____
Date: _____ Time: _____
Reason for Visit: _____

Your Favorite Name(s) for this Room?
- ☐ Powder Room
- ☐ Crapper
- ☐ John
- ☐ The office
- ☐ Can
- ☐ Other....

During Your Visit Did you...
- ☐ Play with your smartphone?
- ☐ Mess with your hair?
- ☐ Inspect your teeth for food?
- ☐ Check out your butt in the mirror?
- ☐ Check your zipper/fly?
- ☐ Read through this entire guest book?

Please Tick All That Apply
- ☐ I take restroom selfies
- ☐ I snoop in medicine cabinets
- ☐ I text/call while on the toilet
- ☐ I pick my nose in the restroom
- ☐ I talk to myself while on the toilet

Doodles & Brilliant Thoughts Inspired by the Throne

 # Welcome to our Restroom
Please Seat Yourself!

Name: _____
Visiting From: _____
Date: _____ Time: _____
Reason for Visit: _____

Your Favorite Name(s) for this Room?
- ☐ Powder Room
- ☐ Crapper
- ☐ John
- ☐ The office
- ☐ Can
- ☐ Other....

During Your Visit Did you...
- ☐ Play with your smartphone?
- ☐ Mess with your hair?
- ☐ Inspect your teeth for food?
- ☐ Check out your butt in the mirror?
- ☐ Check your zipper/fly?
- ☐ Read through this entire guest book?

Please Tick All That Apply
- ☐ I take restroom selfies
- ☐ I snoop in medicine cabinets
- ☐ I text/call while on the toilet
- ☐ I pick my nose in the restroom
- ☐ I talk to myself while on the toilet

Doodles & Brilliant Thoughts Inspired by the Throne

Welcome to our Restroom
Please Seat Yourself!

Name: _____
Visiting From: _____
Date: _____ Time: _____
Reason for Visit: _____

Your Favorite Name(s) for this Room?
- ☐ Powder Room
- ☐ Crapper
- ☐ John
- ☐ The office
- ☐ Can
- ☐ Other....

During Your Visit Did you...
- ☐ Play with your smartphone?
- ☐ Mess with your hair?
- ☐ Inspect your teeth for food?
- ☐ Check out your butt in the mirror?
- ☐ Check your zipper/fly?
- ☐ Read through this entire guest book?

Please Tick All That Apply
- ☐ I take restroom selfies
- ☐ I snoop in medicine cabinets
- ☐ I text/call while on the toilet
- ☐ I pick my nose in the restroom
- ☐ I talk to myself while on the toilet

Doodles & Brilliant Thoughts Inspired by the Throne

Welcome to our Restroom
Please Seat Yourself!

Name: _____
Visiting From: _____
Date: _____ Time: _____
Reason for Visit: _____

Your Favorite Name(s) for this Room?
- ☐ Powder Room
- ☐ Crapper
- ☐ John
- ☐ The office
- ☐ Can
- ☐ Other....

During Your Visit Did you...
- ☐ Play with your smartphone?
- ☐ Mess with your hair?
- ☐ Inspect your teeth for food?
- ☐ Check out your butt in the mirror?
- ☐ Check your zipper/fly?
- ☐ Read through this entire guest book?

Please Tick All That Apply
- ☐ I take restroom selfies
- ☐ I snoop in medicine cabinets
- ☐ I text/call while on the toilet
- ☐ I pick my nose in the restroom
- ☐ I talk to myself while on the toilet

Doodles & Brilliant Thoughts Inspired by the Throne

 # Welcome to our Restroom
Please Seat Yourself!

Name: _____
Visiting From: _____
Date: _____ Time: _____
Reason for Visit: _____

Your Favorite Name(s) for this Room?
- ☐ Powder Room
- ☐ The office
- ☐ Crapper
- ☐ Can
- ☐ John
- ☐ Other....

During Your Visit Did you...
- ☐ Play with your smartphone?
- ☐ Mess with your hair?
- ☐ Inspect your teeth for food?
- ☐ Check out your butt in the mirror?
- ☐ Check your zipper/fly?
- ☐ Read through this entire guest book?

Please Tick All That Apply
- ☐ I take restroom selfies
- ☐ I snoop in medicine cabinets
- ☐ I text/call while on the toilet
- ☐ I pick my nose in the restroom
- ☐ I talk to myself while on the toilet

Doodles & Brilliant Thoughts Inspired by the Throne

Welcome to our Restroom
Please Seat Yourself!

Name: _____
Visiting From: _____
Date: _____ Time: _____
Reason for Visit: _____

Your Favorite Name(s) for this Room?
- ☐ Powder Room
- ☐ Crapper
- ☐ John
- ☐ The office
- ☐ Can
- ☐ Other....

During Your Visit Did you...
- ☐ Play with your smartphone?
- ☐ Mess with your hair?
- ☐ Inspect your teeth for food?
- ☐ Check out your butt in the mirror?
- ☐ Check your zipper/fly?
- ☐ Read through this entire guest book?

Please Tick All That Apply
- ☐ I take restroom selfies
- ☐ I snoop in medicine cabinets
- ☐ I text/call while on the toilet
- ☐ I pick my nose in the restroom
- ☐ I talk to myself while on the toilet

Doodles & Brilliant Thoughts Inspired by the Throne

 # Welcome to our Restroom
Please Seat Yourself!

Name: _____
Visiting From: _____
Date: _____ Time: _____
Reason for Visit: _____

Your Favorite Name(s) for this Room?
- ☐ Powder Room
- ☐ Crapper
- ☐ John
- ☐ The office
- ☐ Can
- ☐ Other....

During Your Visit Did you...
- ☐ Play with your smartphone?
- ☐ Mess with your hair?
- ☐ Inspect your teeth for food?
- ☐ Check out your butt in the mirror?
- ☐ Check your zipper/fly?
- ☐ Read through this entire guest book?

Please Tick All That Apply
- ☐ I take restroom selfies
- ☐ I snoop in medicine cabinets
- ☐ I text/call while on the toilet
- ☐ I pick my nose in the restroom
- ☐ I talk to myself while on the toilet

Doodles & Brilliant Thoughts Inspired by the Throne

 # Welcome to our Restroom
Please Seat Yourself!

Name: _____
Visiting From: _____
Date: _____ Time: _____
Reason for Visit: _____

Your Favorite Name(s) for this Room?
- ☐ Powder Room ☐ The office
- ☐ Crapper   ☐ Can
- ☐ John   ☐ Other....

During Your Visit Did you...
- ☐ Play with your smartphone?
- ☐ Mess with your hair?
- ☐ Inspect your teeth for food?
- ☐ Check out your butt in the mirror?
- ☐ Check your zipper/fly?
- ☐ Read through this entire guest book?

Please Tick All That Apply
- ☐ I take restroom selfies
- ☐ I snoop in medicine cabinets
- ☐ I text/call while on the toilet
- ☐ I pick my nose in the restroom
- ☐ I talk to myself while on the toilet

Doodles & Brilliant Thoughts Inspired by the Throne

Welcome to our Restroom
Please Seat Yourself!

Name: _____
Visiting From: _____
Date: _____ Time: _____
Reason for Visit: _____

Your Favorite Name(s) for this Room?
- ☐ Powder Room
- ☐ Crapper
- ☐ John
- ☐ The office
- ☐ Can
- ☐ Other....

During Your Visit Did you...
- ☐ Play with your smartphone?
- ☐ Mess with your hair?
- ☐ Inspect your teeth for food?
- ☐ Check out your butt in the mirror?
- ☐ Check your zipper/fly?
- ☐ Read through this entire guest book?

Please Tick All That Apply
- ☐ I take restroom selfies
- ☐ I snoop in medicine cabinets
- ☐ I text/call while on the toilet
- ☐ I pick my nose in the restroom
- ☐ I talk to myself while on the toilet

Doodles & Brilliant Thoughts Inspired by the Throne

Welcome to our Restroom
Please Seat Yourself!

Name: _____
Visiting From: _____
Date: _____ Time: _____
Reason for Visit: _____

Your Favorite Name(s) for this Room?
- ☐ Powder Room
- ☐ Crapper
- ☐ John
- ☐ The office
- ☐ Can
- ☐ Other....

During Your Visit Did you...
- ☐ Play with your smartphone?
- ☐ Mess with your hair?
- ☐ Inspect your teeth for food?
- ☐ Check out your butt in the mirror?
- ☐ Check your zipper/fly?
- ☐ Read through this entire guest book?

Please Tick All That Apply
- ☐ I take restroom selfies
- ☐ I snoop in medicine cabinets
- ☐ I text/call while on the toilet
- ☐ I pick my nose in the restroom
- ☐ I talk to myself while on the toilet

Doodles & Brilliant Thoughts Inspired by the Throne

Welcome to our Restroom
Please Seat Yourself!

Name: _____
Visiting From: _____
Date: _____ Time: _____
Reason for Visit: _____

Your Favorite Name(s) for this Room?
- ☐ Powder Room
- ☐ Crapper
- ☐ John
- ☐ The office
- ☐ Can
- ☐ Other....

During Your Visit Did you...
- ☐ Play with your smartphone?
- ☐ Mess with your hair?
- ☐ Inspect your teeth for food?
- ☐ Check out your butt in the mirror?
- ☐ Check your zipper/fly?
- ☐ Read through this entire guest book?

Please Tick All That Apply
- ☐ I take restroom selfies
- ☐ I snoop in medicine cabinets
- ☐ I text/call while on the toilet
- ☐ I pick my nose in the restroom
- ☐ I talk to myself while on the toilet

Doodles & Brilliant Thoughts Inspired by the Throne

Welcome to our Restroom
Please Seat Yourself!

Name: _____
Visiting From: _____
Date: _____ Time: _____
Reason for Visit: _____

Your Favorite Name(s) for this Room?
- ☐ Powder Room
- ☐ Crapper
- ☐ John
- ☐ The office
- ☐ Can
- ☐ Other....

During Your Visit Did you...
- ☐ Play with your smartphone?
- ☐ Mess with your hair?
- ☐ Inspect your teeth for food?
- ☐ Check out your butt in the mirror?
- ☐ Check your zipper/fly?
- ☐ Read through this entire guest book?

Please Tick All That Apply
- ☐ I take restroom selfies
- ☐ I snoop in medicine cabinets
- ☐ I text/call while on the toilet
- ☐ I pick my nose in the restroom
- ☐ I talk to myself while on the toilet

Doodles & Brilliant Thoughts Inspired by the Throne

Welcome to our Restroom
Please Seat Yourself!

Name: _____
Visiting From: _____
Date: _____ Time: _____
Reason for Visit: _____

Your Favorite Name(s) for this Room?
- ☐ Powder Room
- ☐ Crapper
- ☐ John
- ☐ The office
- ☐ Can
- ☐ Other....

During Your Visit Did you...
- ☐ Play with your smartphone?
- ☐ Mess with your hair?
- ☐ Inspect your teeth for food?
- ☐ Check out your butt in the mirror?
- ☐ Check your zipper/fly?
- ☐ Read through this entire guest book?

Please Tick All That Apply
- ☐ I take restroom selfies
- ☐ I snoop in medicine cabinets
- ☐ I text/call while on the toilet
- ☐ I pick my nose in the restroom
- ☐ I talk to myself while on the toilet

Doodles & Brilliant Thoughts Inspired by the Throne

Welcome to our Restroom
Please Seat Yourself!

Name: _____
Visiting From: _____
Date: _____ Time: _____
Reason for Visit: _____

Your Favorite Name(s) for this Room?
- ☐ Powder Room
- ☐ Crapper
- ☐ John
- ☐ The office
- ☐ Can
- ☐ Other....

During Your Visit Did you...
- ☐ Play with your smartphone?
- ☐ Mess with your hair?
- ☐ Inspect your teeth for food?
- ☐ Check out your butt in the mirror?
- ☐ Check your zipper/fly?
- ☐ Read through this entire guest book?

Please Tick All That Apply
- ☐ I take restroom selfies
- ☐ I snoop in medicine cabinets
- ☐ I text/call while on the toilet
- ☐ I pick my nose in the restroom
- ☐ I talk to myself while on the toilet

Doodles & Brilliant Thoughts Inspired by the Throne

Welcome to our Restroom
Please Seat Yourself!

Name: _____
Visiting From: _____
Date: _____ Time: _____
Reason for Visit: _____

Your Favorite Name(s) for this Room?
- ☐ Powder Room
- ☐ Crapper
- ☐ John
- ☐ The office
- ☐ Can
- ☐ Other....

During Your Visit Did you...
- ☐ Play with your smartphone?
- ☐ Mess with your hair?
- ☐ Inspect your teeth for food?
- ☐ Check out your butt in the mirror?
- ☐ Check your zipper/fly?
- ☐ Read through this entire guest book?

Please Tick All That Apply
- ☐ I take restroom selfies
- ☐ I snoop in medicine cabinets
- ☐ I text/call while on the toilet
- ☐ I pick my nose in the restroom
- ☐ I talk to myself while on the toilet

Doodles & Brilliant Thoughts Inspired by the Throne

Welcome to our Restroom
Please Seat Yourself!

Name: _____
Visiting From: _____
Date: _____ Time: _____
Reason for Visit: _____

Your Favorite Name(s) for this Room?
- ☐ Powder Room
- ☐ Crapper
- ☐ John
- ☐ The office
- ☐ Can
- ☐ Other....

During Your Visit Did you...
- ☐ Play with your smartphone?
- ☐ Mess with your hair?
- ☐ Inspect your teeth for food?
- ☐ Check out your butt in the mirror?
- ☐ Check your zipper/fly?
- ☐ Read through this entire guest book?

Please Tick All That Apply
- ☐ I take restroom selfies
- ☐ I snoop in medicine cabinets
- ☐ I text/call while on the toilet
- ☐ I pick my nose in the restroom
- ☐ I talk to myself while on the toilet

Doodles & Brilliant Thoughts Inspired by the Throne

 # Welcome to our Restroom
Please Seat Yourself!

Name: _____
Visiting From: _____
Date: _____ Time: _____
Reason for Visit: _____

Your Favorite Name(s) for this Room?
- ☐ Powder Room
- ☐ Crapper
- ☐ John
- ☐ The office
- ☐ Can
- ☐ Other....

During Your Visit Did you...
- ☐ Play with your smartphone?
- ☐ Mess with your hair?
- ☐ Inspect your teeth for food?
- ☐ Check out your butt in the mirror?
- ☐ Check your zipper/fly?
- ☐ Read through this entire guest book?

Please Tick All That Apply
- ☐ I take restroom selfies
- ☐ I snoop in medicine cabinets
- ☐ I text/call while on the toilet
- ☐ I pick my nose in the restroom
- ☐ I talk to myself while on the toilet

Doodles & Brilliant Thoughts Inspired by the Throne

Welcome to our Restroom
Please Seat Yourself!

Name: _____
Visiting From: _____
Date: _____ Time: _____
Reason for Visit: _____

Your Favorite Name(s) for this Room?
- ☐ Powder Room
- ☐ Crapper
- ☐ John
- ☐ The Office
- ☐ Can
- ☐ Other....

During Your Visit Did you...
- ☐ Play with your smartphone?
- ☐ Mess with your hair?
- ☐ Inspect your teeth for food?
- ☐ Check out your butt in the mirror?
- ☐ Check your zipper/fly?
- ☐ Read through this entire guest book?

Please Tick All That Apply
- ☐ I take restroom selfies
- ☐ I snoop in medicine cabinets
- ☐ I text/call while on the toilet
- ☐ I pick my nose in the restroom
- ☐ I talk to myself while on the toilet

Doodles & Brilliant Thoughts Inspired by the Throne

Welcome to our Restroom
Please Seat Yourself!

Name: _____
Visiting From: _____
Date: _____ Time: _____
Reason for Visit: _____

Your Favorite Name(s) for this Room?
- ☐ Powder Room
- ☐ Crapper
- ☐ John
- ☐ The office
- ☐ Can
- ☐ Other....

During Your Visit Did you...
- ☐ Play with your smartphone?
- ☐ Mess with your hair?
- ☐ Inspect your teeth for food?
- ☐ Check out your butt in the mirror?
- ☐ Check your zipper/fly?
- ☐ Read through this entire guest book?

Please Tick All That Apply
- ☐ I take restroom selfies
- ☐ I snoop in medicine cabinets
- ☐ I text/call while on the toilet
- ☐ I pick my nose in the restroom
- ☐ I talk to myself while on the toilet

Doodles & Brilliant Thoughts Inspired by the Throne

Welcome to our Restroom
Please Seat Yourself!

Name: ───────────────
Visiting From: ───────────────
Date: ──────── Time: ────────
Reason for Visit: ───────────────

Your Favorite Name(s) for this Room?
- ☐ Powder Room
- ☐ Crapper
- ☐ John
- ☐ The office
- ☐ Can
- ☐ Other....

During Your Visit Did you...
- ☐ Play with your smartphone?
- ☐ Mess with your hair?
- ☐ Inspect your teeth for food?
- ☐ Check out your butt in the mirror?
- ☐ Check your zipper/fly?
- ☐ Read through this entire guest book?

Please Tick All That Apply
- ☐ I take restroom selfies
- ☐ I snoop in medicine cabinets
- ☐ I text/call while on the toilet
- ☐ I pick my nose in the restroom
- ☐ I talk to myself while on the toilet

Doodles & Brilliant Thoughts Inspired by the Throne

Welcome to our Restroom
Please Seat Yourself!

Name: _____
Visiting From: _____
Date: _____ Time: _____
Reason for Visit: _____

Your Favorite Name(s) for this Room?
- ☐ Powder Room
- ☐ Crapper
- ☐ John
- ☐ The office
- ☐ Can
- ☐ Other....

During Your Visit Did you...
- ☐ Play with your smartphone?
- ☐ Mess with your hair?
- ☐ Inspect your teeth for food?
- ☐ Check out your butt in the mirror?
- ☐ Check your zipper/fly?
- ☐ Read through this entire guest book?

Please Tick All That Apply
- ☐ I take restroom selfies
- ☐ I snoop in medicine cabinets
- ☐ I text/call while on the toilet
- ☐ I pick my nose in the restroom
- ☐ I talk to myself while on the toilet

Doodles & Brilliant Thoughts Inspired by the Throne

Welcome to our Restroom
Please Seat Yourself!

Name: _____
Visiting From: _____
Date: _____ Time: _____
Reason for Visit: _____

Your Favorite Name(s) for this Room?
- ☐ Powder Room
- ☐ Crapper
- ☐ John
- ☐ The office
- ☐ Can
- ☐ Other....

During Your Visit Did you...
- ☐ Play with your smartphone?
- ☐ Mess with your hair?
- ☐ Inspect your teeth for food?
- ☐ Check out your butt in the mirror?
- ☐ Check your zipper/fly?
- ☐ Read through this entire guest book?

Please Tick All That Apply
- ☐ I take restroom selfies
- ☐ I snoop in medicine cabinets
- ☐ I text/call while on the toilet
- ☐ I pick my nose in the restroom
- ☐ I talk to myself while on the toilet

Doodles & Brilliant Thoughts Inspired by the Throne

Welcome to our Restroom
Please Seat Yourself!

Name: _____
Visiting From: _____
Date: _____ Time: _____
Reason for Visit: _____

Your Favorite Name(s) for this Room?
- ☐ Powder Room
- ☐ Crapper
- ☐ John
- ☐ The office
- ☐ Can
- ☐ Other....

During Your Visit Did you...
- ☐ Play with your smartphone?
- ☐ Mess with your hair?
- ☐ Inspect your teeth for food?
- ☐ Check out your butt in the mirror?
- ☐ Check your zipper/fly?
- ☐ Read through this entire guest book?

Please Tick All That Apply
- ☐ I take restroom selfies
- ☐ I snoop in medicine cabinets
- ☐ I text/call while on the toilet
- ☐ I pick my nose in the restroom
- ☐ I talk to myself while on the toilet

Doodles & Brilliant Thoughts Inspired by the Throne

Welcome to our Restroom
Please Seat Yourself!

Name: _____
Visiting From: _____
Date: _____ Time: _____
Reason for Visit: _____

Your Favorite Name(s) for this Room?
- ☐ Powder Room
- ☐ Crapper
- ☐ John
- ☐ The office
- ☐ Can
- ☐ Other....

During Your Visit Did you...
- ☐ Play with your smartphone?
- ☐ Mess with your hair?
- ☐ Inspect your teeth for food?
- ☐ Check out your butt in the mirror?
- ☐ Check your zipper/fly?
- ☐ Read through this entire guest book?

Please Tick All That Apply
- ☐ I take restroom selfies
- ☐ I snoop in medicine cabinets
- ☐ I text/call while on the toilet
- ☐ I pick my nose in the restroom
- ☐ I talk to myself while on the toilet

Doodles & Brilliant Thoughts Inspired by the Throne

Welcome to our Restroom
Please Seat Yourself!

Name: _____
Visiting From: _____
Date: _____ Time: _____
Reason for Visit: _____

Your Favorite Name(s) for this Room?
- ☐ Powder Room
- ☐ Crapper
- ☐ John
- ☐ The office
- ☐ Can
- ☐ Other….

During Your Visit Did you…
- ☐ Play with your smartphone?
- ☐ Mess with your hair?
- ☐ Inspect your teeth for food?
- ☐ Check out your butt in the mirror?
- ☐ Check your zipper/fly?
- ☐ Read through this entire guest book?

Please Tick All That Apply
- ☐ I take restroom selfies
- ☐ I snoop in medicine cabinets
- ☐ I text/call while on the toilet
- ☐ I pick my nose in the restroom
- ☐ I talk to myself while on the toilet

Doodles & Brilliant Thoughts Inspired by the Throne

Welcome to our Restroom
Please Seat Yourself!

Name: _____
Visiting From: _____
Date: _____ Time: _____
Reason for Visit: _____

Your Favorite Name(s) for this Room?
- ☐ Powder Room
- ☐ Crapper
- ☐ John
- ☐ The office
- ☐ Can
- ☐ Other....

During Your Visit Did you...
- ☐ Play with your smartphone?
- ☐ Mess with your hair?
- ☐ Inspect your teeth for food?
- ☐ Check out your butt in the mirror?
- ☐ Check your zipper/fly?
- ☐ Read through this entire guest book?

Please Tick All That Apply
- ☐ I take restroom selfies
- ☐ I snoop in medicine cabinets
- ☐ I text/call while on the toilet
- ☐ I pick my nose in the restroom
- ☐ I talk to myself while on the toilet

Doodles & Brilliant Thoughts Inspired by the Throne

Welcome to our Restroom
Please Seat Yourself!

Name: _____
Visiting From: _____
Date: _____ Time: _____
Reason for Visit: _____

Your Favorite Name(s) for this Room?
- ☐ Powder Room
- ☐ Crapper
- ☐ John
- ☐ The office
- ☐ Can
- ☐ Other….

During Your Visit Did you…
- ☐ Play with your smartphone?
- ☐ Mess with your hair?
- ☐ Inspect your teeth for food?
- ☐ Check out your butt in the mirror?
- ☐ Check your zipper/fly?
- ☐ Read through this entire guest book?

Please Tick All That Apply
- ☐ I take restroom selfies
- ☐ I snoop in medicine cabinets
- ☐ I text/call while on the toilet
- ☐ I pick my nose in the restroom
- ☐ I talk to myself while on the toilet

Doodles & Brilliant Thoughts Inspired by the Throne

Welcome to our Restroom
Please Seat Yourself!

Name: _____
Visiting From: _____
Date: _____ Time: _____
Reason for Visit: _____

Your Favorite Name(s) for this Room?
- ☐ Powder Room
- ☐ Crapper
- ☐ John
- ☐ The office
- ☐ Can
- ☐ Other....

During Your Visit Did you...
- ☐ Play with your smartphone?
- ☐ Mess with your hair?
- ☐ Inspect your teeth for food?
- ☐ Check out your butt in the mirror?
- ☐ Check your zipper/fly?
- ☐ Read through this entire guest book?

Please Tick All That Apply
- ☐ I take restroom selfies
- ☐ I snoop in medicine cabinets
- ☐ I text/call while on the toilet
- ☐ I pick my nose in the restroom
- ☐ I talk to myself while on the toilet

Doodles & Brilliant Thoughts Inspired by the Throne

Welcome to our Restroom
Please Seat Yourself!

Name: _____
Visiting From: _____
Date: _____ Time: _____
Reason for Visit: _____

Your Favorite Name(s) for this Room?
- ☐ Powder Room
- ☐ Crapper
- ☐ John
- ☐ The office
- ☐ Can
- ☐ Other....

During Your Visit Did you...
- ☐ Play with your smartphone?
- ☐ Mess with your hair?
- ☐ Inspect your teeth for food?
- ☐ Check out your butt in the mirror?
- ☐ Check your zipper/fly?
- ☐ Read through this entire guest book?

Please Tick All That Apply
- ☐ I take restroom selfies
- ☐ I snoop in medicine cabinets
- ☐ I text/call while on the toilet
- ☐ I pick my nose in the restroom
- ☐ I talk to myself while on the toilet

Doodles & Brilliant Thoughts Inspired by the Throne

 # Welcome to our Restroom
Please Seat Yourself!

Name: _____
Visiting From: _____
Date: _____ Time: _____
Reason for Visit: _____

Your Favorite Name(s) for this Room?
- ☐ Powder Room
- ☐ Crapper
- ☐ John
- ☐ The office
- ☐ Can
- ☐ Other....

During Your Visit Did you...
- ☐ Play with your smartphone?
- ☐ Mess with your hair?
- ☐ Inspect your teeth for food?
- ☐ Check out your butt in the mirror?
- ☐ Check your zipper/fly?
- ☐ Read through this entire guest book?

Please Tick All That Apply
- ☐ I take restroom selfies
- ☐ I snoop in medicine cabinets
- ☐ I text/call while on the toilet
- ☐ I pick my nose in the restroom
- ☐ I talk to myself while on the toilet

Doodles & Brilliant Thoughts Inspired by the Throne

Welcome to our Restroom
Please Seat Yourself!

Name: _____
Visiting From: _____
Date: _____ Time: _____
Reason for Visit: _____

Your Favorite Name(s) for this Room?
- ☐ Powder Room
- ☐ Crapper
- ☐ John
- ☐ The office
- ☐ Can
- ☐ Other....

During Your Visit Did you...
- ☐ Play with your smartphone?
- ☐ Mess with your hair?
- ☐ Inspect your teeth for food?
- ☐ Check out your butt in the mirror?
- ☐ Check your zipper/fly?
- ☐ Read through this entire guest book?

Please Tick All That Apply
- ☐ I take restroom selfies
- ☐ I snoop in medicine cabinets
- ☐ I text/call while on the toilet
- ☐ I pick my nose in the restroom
- ☐ I talk to myself while on the toilet

Doodles & Brilliant Thoughts Inspired by the Throne

Welcome to our Restroom
Please Seat Yourself!

Name: _____
Visiting From: _____
Date: _____ Time: _____
Reason for Visit: _____

Your Favorite Name(s) for this Room?
- ☐ Powder Room
- ☐ The office
- ☐ Crapper
- ☐ Can
- ☐ John
- ☐ Other....

During Your Visit Did you...
- ☐ Play with your smartphone?
- ☐ Mess with your hair?
- ☐ Inspect your teeth for food?
- ☐ Check out your butt in the mirror?
- ☐ Check your zipper/fly?
- ☐ Read through this entire guest book?

Please Tick All That Apply
- ☐ I take restroom selfies
- ☐ I snoop in medicine cabinets
- ☐ I text/call while on the toilet
- ☐ I pick my nose in the restroom
- ☐ I talk to myself while on the toilet

Doodles & Brilliant Thoughts Inspired by the Throne

Welcome to our Restroom
Please Seat Yourself!

Name: _____
Visiting From: _____
Date: _____ Time: _____
Reason for Visit: _____

Your Favorite Name(s) for this Room?
- ☐ Powder Room
- ☐ Crapper
- ☐ John
- ☐ The office
- ☐ Can
- ☐ Other....

During Your Visit Did you...
- ☐ Play with your smartphone?
- ☐ Mess with your hair?
- ☐ Inspect your teeth for food?
- ☐ Check out your butt in the mirror?
- ☐ Check your zipper/fly?
- ☐ Read through this entire guest book?

Please Tick All That Apply
- ☐ I take restroom selfies
- ☐ I snoop in medicine cabinets
- ☐ I text/call while on the toilet
- ☐ I pick my nose in the restroom
- ☐ I talk to myself while on the toilet

Doodles & Brilliant Thoughts Inspired by the Throne

 # Welcome to our Restroom
Please Seat Yourself!

Name: _____
Visiting From: _____
Date: _____ Time: _____
Reason for Visit: _____

Your Favorite Name(s) for this Room?
- ☐ Powder Room
- ☐ Crapper
- ☐ John
- ☐ The office
- ☐ Can
- ☐ Other....

During Your Visit Did you...
- ☐ Play with your smartphone?
- ☐ Mess with your hair?
- ☐ Inspect your teeth for food?
- ☐ Check out your butt in the mirror?
- ☐ Check your zipper/fly?
- ☐ Read through this entire guest book?

Please Tick All That Apply
- ☐ I take restroom selfies
- ☐ I snoop in medicine cabinets
- ☐ I text/call while on the toilet
- ☐ I pick my nose in the restroom
- ☐ I talk to myself while on the toilet

Doodles & Brilliant Thoughts Inspired by the Throne

Welcome to our Restroom
Please Seat Yourself!

Name: _____
Visiting From: _____
Date: _____ Time: _____
Reason for Visit: _____

Your Favorite Name(s) for this Room?
- ☐ Powder Room
- ☐ Crapper
- ☐ John
- ☐ The office
- ☐ Can
- ☐ Other....

During Your Visit Did you...
- ☐ Play with your smartphone?
- ☐ Mess with your hair?
- ☐ Inspect your teeth for food?
- ☐ Check out your butt in the mirror?
- ☐ Check your zipper/fly?
- ☐ Read through this entire guest book?

Please Tick All That Apply
- ☐ I take restroom selfies
- ☐ I snoop in medicine cabinets
- ☐ I text/call while on the toilet
- ☐ I pick my nose in the restroom
- ☐ I talk to myself while on the toilet

Doodles & Brilliant Thoughts Inspired by the Throne

Welcome to our Restroom
Please Seat Yourself!

Name: _____
Visiting From: _____
Date: _____ Time: _____
Reason for Visit: _____

Your Favorite Name(s) for this Room?
- ☐ Powder Room
- ☐ Crapper
- ☐ John
- ☐ The office
- ☐ Can
- ☐ Other....

During Your Visit Did you...
- ☐ Play with your smartphone?
- ☐ Mess with your hair?
- ☐ Inspect your teeth for food?
- ☐ Check out your butt in the mirror?
- ☐ Check your zipper/fly?
- ☐ Read through this entire guest book?

Please Tick All That Apply
- ☐ I take restroom selfies
- ☐ I snoop in medicine cabinets
- ☐ I text/call while on the toilet
- ☐ I pick my nose in the restroom
- ☐ I talk to myself while on the toilet

Doodles & Brilliant Thoughts Inspired by the Throne

Welcome to our Restroom
Please Seat Yourself!

Name: _____
Visiting From: _____
Date: _____ Time: _____
Reason for Visit: _____

Your Favorite Name(s) for this Room?
- ☐ Powder Room
- ☐ Crapper
- ☐ John
- ☐ The office
- ☐ Can
- ☐ Other....

During Your Visit Did you...
- ☐ Play with your smartphone?
- ☐ Mess with your hair?
- ☐ Inspect your teeth for food?
- ☐ Check out your butt in the mirror?
- ☐ Check your zipper/fly?
- ☐ Read through this entire guest book?

Please Tick All That Apply
- ☐ I take restroom selfies
- ☐ I snoop in medicine cabinets
- ☐ I text/call while on the toilet
- ☐ I pick my nose in the restroom
- ☐ I talk to myself while on the toilet

Doodles & Brilliant Thoughts Inspired by the Throne

Welcome to our Restroom
Please Seat Yourself!

Name: _____
Visiting From: _____
Date: _____ Time: _____
Reason for Visit: _____

Your Favorite Name(s) for this Room?
- ☐ Powder Room
- ☐ Crapper
- ☐ John
- ☐ The office
- ☐ Can
- ☐ Other....

During Your Visit Did you...
- ☐ Play with your smartphone?
- ☐ Mess with your hair?
- ☐ Inspect your teeth for food?
- ☐ Check out your butt in the mirror?
- ☐ Check your zipper/fly?
- ☐ Read through this entire guest book?

Please Tick All That Apply
- ☐ I take restroom selfies
- ☐ I snoop in medicine cabinets
- ☐ I text/call while on the toilet
- ☐ I pick my nose in the restroom
- ☐ I talk to myself while on the toilet

Doodles & Brilliant Thoughts Inspired by the Throne

Welcome to our Restroom
Please Seat Yourself!

Name: _____
Visiting From: _____
Date: _____ Time: _____
Reason for Visit: _____

Your Favorite Name(s) for this Room?
- ☐ Powder Room
- ☐ Crapper
- ☐ John
- ☐ The office
- ☐ Can
- ☐ Other....

During Your Visit Did you...
- ☐ Play with your smartphone?
- ☐ Mess with your hair?
- ☐ Inspect your teeth for food?
- ☐ Check out your butt in the mirror?
- ☐ Check your zipper/fly?
- ☐ Read through this entire guest book?

Please Tick All That Apply
- ☐ I take restroom selfies
- ☐ I snoop in medicine cabinets
- ☐ I text/call while on the toilet
- ☐ I pick my nose in the restroom
- ☐ I talk to myself while on the toilet

Doodles & Brilliant Thoughts Inspired by the Throne

Welcome to our Restroom
Please Seat Yourself!

Name: _____
Visiting From: _____
Date: _____ Time: _____
Reason for Visit: _____

Your Favorite Name(s) for this Room?
- ☐ Powder Room
- ☐ Crapper
- ☐ John
- ☐ The office
- ☐ Can
- ☐ Other....

During Your Visit Did you...
- ☐ Play with your smartphone?
- ☐ Mess with your hair?
- ☐ Inspect your teeth for food?
- ☐ Check out your butt in the mirror?
- ☐ Check your zipper/fly?
- ☐ Read through this entire guest book?

Please Tick All That Apply
- ☐ I take restroom selfies
- ☐ I snoop in medicine cabinets
- ☐ I text/call while on the toilet
- ☐ I pick my nose in the restroom
- ☐ I talk to myself while on the toilet

Doodles & Brilliant Thoughts Inspired by the Throne

Welcome to our Restroom
Please Seat Yourself!

Name: _____
Visiting From: _____
Date: _____ Time: _____
Reason for Visit: _____

Your Favorite Name(s) for this Room?
- ☐ Powder Room
- ☐ Crapper
- ☐ John
- ☐ The office
- ☐ Can
- ☐ Other....

During Your Visit Did you...
- ☐ Play with your smartphone?
- ☐ Mess with your hair?
- ☐ Inspect your teeth for food?
- ☐ Check out your butt in the mirror?
- ☐ Check your zipper/fly?
- ☐ Read through this entire guest book?

Please Tick All That Apply
- ☐ I take restroom selfies
- ☐ I snoop in medicine cabinets
- ☐ I text/call while on the toilet
- ☐ I pick my nose in the restroom
- ☐ I talk to myself while on the toilet

Doodles & Brilliant Thoughts Inspired by the Throne

 # Welcome to our Restroom
Please Seat Yourself!

Name: _____
Visiting From: _____
Date: _____ Time: _____
Reason for Visit: _____

Your Favorite Name(s) for this Room?
- ☐ Powder Room
- ☐ Crapper
- ☐ John
- ☐ The office
- ☐ Can
- ☐ Other....

During Your Visit Did you...
- ☐ Play with your smartphone?
- ☐ Mess with your hair?
- ☐ Inspect your teeth for food?
- ☐ Check out your butt in the mirror?
- ☐ Check your zipper/fly?
- ☐ Read through this entire guest book?

Please Tick All That Apply
- ☐ I take restroom selfies
- ☐ I snoop in medicine cabinets
- ☐ I text/call while on the toilet
- ☐ I pick my nose in the restroom
- ☐ I talk to myself while on the toilet

Doodles & Brilliant Thoughts Inspired by the Throne

Welcome to our Restroom
Please Seat Yourself!

Name: _____
Visiting From: _____
Date: _____ Time: _____
Reason for Visit: _____

Your Favorite Name(s) for this Room?
- ☐ Powder Room
- ☐ Crapper
- ☐ John
- ☐ The office
- ☐ Can
- ☐ Other....

During Your Visit Did you...
- ☐ Play with your smartphone?
- ☐ Mess with your hair?
- ☐ Inspect your teeth for food?
- ☐ Check out your butt in the mirror?
- ☐ Check your zipper/fly?
- ☐ Read through this entire guest book?

Please Tick All That Apply
- ☐ I take restroom selfies
- ☐ I snoop in medicine cabinets
- ☐ I text/call while on the toilet
- ☐ I pick my nose in the restroom
- ☐ I talk to myself while on the toilet

Doodles & Brilliant Thoughts Inspired by the Throne

Welcome to our Restroom
Please Seat Yourself!

Name: _____
Visiting From: _____
Date: _____ Time: _____
Reason for Visit: _____

Your Favorite Name(s) for this Room?
- ☐ Powder Room
- ☐ Crapper
- ☐ John
- ☐ The office
- ☐ Can
- ☐ Other....

During Your Visit Did you...
- ☐ Play with your smartphone?
- ☐ Mess with your hair?
- ☐ Inspect your teeth for food?
- ☐ Check out your butt in the mirror?
- ☐ Check your zipper/fly?
- ☐ Read through this entire guest book?

Please Tick All That Apply
- ☐ I take restroom selfies
- ☐ I snoop in medicine cabinets
- ☐ I text/call while on the toilet
- ☐ I pick my nose in the restroom
- ☐ I talk to myself while on the toilet

Doodles & Brilliant Thoughts Inspired by the Throne

Welcome to our Restroom
Please Seat Yourself!

Name: _____
Visiting From: _____
Date: _____ Time: _____
Reason for Visit: _____

Your Favorite Name(s) for this Room?
- ☐ Powder Room
- ☐ Crapper
- ☐ John
- ☐ The office
- ☐ Can
- ☐ Other....

During Your Visit Did you...
- ☐ Play with your smartphone?
- ☐ Mess with your hair?
- ☐ Inspect your teeth for food?
- ☐ Check out your butt in the mirror?
- ☐ Check your zipper/fly?
- ☐ Read through this entire guest book?

Please Tick All That Apply
- ☐ I take restroom selfies
- ☐ I snoop in medicine cabinets
- ☐ I text/call while on the toilet
- ☐ I pick my nose in the restroom
- ☐ I talk to myself while on the toilet

Doodles & Brilliant Thoughts Inspired by the Throne

Welcome to our Restroom
Please Seat Yourself!

Name: _____
Visiting From: _____
Date: _____ Time: _____
Reason for Visit: _____

Your Favorite Name(s) for this Room?
- ☐ Powder Room
- ☐ Crapper
- ☐ John
- ☐ The office
- ☐ Can
- ☐ Other....

During Your Visit Did you...
- ☐ Play with your smartphone?
- ☐ Mess with your hair?
- ☐ Inspect your teeth for food?
- ☐ Check out your butt in the mirror?
- ☐ Check your zipper/fly?
- ☐ Read through this entire guest book?

Please Tick All That Apply
- ☐ I take restroom selfies
- ☐ I snoop in medicine cabinets
- ☐ I text/call while on the toilet
- ☐ I pick my nose in the restroom
- ☐ I talk to myself while on the toilet

Doodles & Brilliant Thoughts Inspired by the Throne

Welcome to our Restroom
Please Seat Yourself!

Name: _____
Visiting From: _____
Date: _____ Time: _____
Reason for Visit: _____

Your Favorite Name(s) for this Room?
- ☐ Powder Room
- ☐ Crapper
- ☐ John
- ☐ The office
- ☐ Can
- ☐ Other....

During Your Visit Did you...
- ☐ Play with your smartphone?
- ☐ Mess with your hair?
- ☐ Inspect your teeth for food?
- ☐ Check out your butt in the mirror?
- ☐ Check your zipper/fly?
- ☐ Read through this entire guest book?

Please Tick All That Apply
- ☐ I take restroom selfies
- ☐ I snoop in medicine cabinets
- ☐ I text/call while on the toilet
- ☐ I pick my nose in the restroom
- ☐ I talk to myself while on the toilet

Doodles & Brilliant Thoughts Inspired by the Throne

Welcome to our Restroom
Please Seat Yourself!

Name: _____
Visiting From: _____
Date: _____ Time: _____
Reason for Visit: _____

Your Favorite Name(s) for this Room?
- ☐ Powder Room
- ☐ The office
- ☐ Crapper
- ☐ Can
- ☐ John
- ☐ Other....

During Your Visit Did you...
- ☐ Play with your smartphone?
- ☐ Mess with your hair?
- ☐ Inspect your teeth for food?
- ☐ Check out your butt in the mirror?
- ☐ Check your zipper/fly?
- ☐ Read through this entire guest book?

Please Tick All That Apply
- ☐ I take restroom selfies
- ☐ I snoop in medicine cabinets
- ☐ I text/call while on the toilet
- ☐ I pick my nose in the restroom
- ☐ I talk to myself while on the toilet

Doodles & Brilliant Thoughts Inspired by the Throne

 # Welcome to our Restroom
Please Seat Yourself!

Name: _____
Visiting From: _____
Date: _____ Time: _____
Reason for Visit: _____

Your Favorite Name(s) for this Room?
- ☐ Powder Room
- ☐ Crapper
- ☐ John
- ☐ The office
- ☐ Can
- ☐ Other....

During Your Visit Did you…
- ☐ Play with your smartphone?
- ☐ Mess with your hair?
- ☐ Inspect your teeth for food?
- ☐ Check out your butt in the mirror?
- ☐ Check your zipper/fly?
- ☐ Read through this entire guest book?

Please Tick All That Apply
- ☐ I take restroom selfies
- ☐ I snoop in medicine cabinets
- ☐ I text/call while on the toilet
- ☐ I pick my nose in the restroom
- ☐ I talk to myself while on the toilet

Doodles & Brilliant Thoughts Inspired by the Throne

Welcome to our Restroom
Please Seat Yourself!

Name: _____
Visiting From: _____
Date: _____ Time: _____
Reason for Visit: _____

Your Favorite Name(s) for this Room?
- ☐ Powder Room
- ☐ Crapper
- ☐ John
- ☐ The office
- ☐ Can
- ☐ Other....

During Your Visit Did you...
- ☐ Play with your smartphone?
- ☐ Mess with your hair?
- ☐ Inspect your teeth for food?
- ☐ Check out your butt in the mirror?
- ☐ Check your zipper/fly?
- ☐ Read through this entire guest book?

Please Tick All That Apply
- ☐ I take restroom selfies
- ☐ I snoop in medicine cabinets
- ☐ I text/call while on the toilet
- ☐ I pick my nose in the restroom
- ☐ I talk to myself while on the toilet

Doodles & Brilliant Thoughts Inspired by the Throne

Welcome to our Restroom
Please Seat Yourself!

Name: _____
Visiting From: _____
Date: _____ Time: _____
Reason for Visit: _____

Your Favorite Name(s) for this Room?
- ☐ Powder Room
- ☐ Crapper
- ☐ John
- ☐ The office
- ☐ Can
- ☐ Other....

During Your Visit Did you...
- ☐ Play with your smartphone?
- ☐ Mess with your hair?
- ☐ Inspect your teeth for food?
- ☐ Check out your butt in the mirror?
- ☐ Check your zipper/fly?
- ☐ Read through this entire guest book?

Please Tick All That Apply
- ☐ I take restroom selfies
- ☐ I snoop in medicine cabinets
- ☐ I text/call while on the toilet
- ☐ I pick my nose in the restroom
- ☐ I talk to myself while on the toilet

Doodles & Brilliant Thoughts Inspired by the Throne

Welcome to our Restroom
Please Seat Yourself!

Name: _____
Visiting From: _____
Date: _____ Time: _____
Reason for Visit: _____

Your Favorite Name(s) for this Room?
- ☐ Powder Room
- ☐ Crapper
- ☐ John
- ☐ The office
- ☐ Can
- ☐ Other....

During Your Visit Did you...
- ☐ Play with your smartphone?
- ☐ Mess with your hair?
- ☐ Inspect your teeth for food?
- ☐ Check out your butt in the mirror?
- ☐ Check your zipper/fly?
- ☐ Read through this entire guest book?

Please Tick All That Apply
- ☐ I take restroom selfies
- ☐ I snoop in medicine cabinets
- ☐ I text/call while on the toilet
- ☐ I pick my nose in the restroom
- ☐ I talk to myself while on the toilet

Doodles & Brilliant Thoughts Inspired by the Throne

 # Welcome to our Restroom
Please Seat Yourself!

Name: _____

Visiting From: _____

Date: _____ Time: _____

Reason for Visit: _____

Your Favorite Name(s) for this Room?
- ☐ Powder Room
- ☐ Crapper
- ☐ John
- ☐ The office
- ☐ Can
- ☐ Other....

During Your Visit Did you...
- ☐ Play with your smartphone?
- ☐ Mess with your hair?
- ☐ Inspect your teeth for food?
- ☐ Check out your butt in the mirror?
- ☐ Check your zipper/fly?
- ☐ Read through this entire guest book?

Please Tick All That Apply
- ☐ I take restroom selfies
- ☐ I snoop in medicine cabinets
- ☐ I text/call while on the toilet
- ☐ I pick my nose in the restroom
- ☐ I talk to myself while on the toilet

Doodles & Brilliant Thoughts Inspired by the Throne

Welcome to our Restroom
Please Seat Yourself!

Name: _____
Visiting From: _____
Date: _____ Time: _____
Reason for Visit: _____

Your Favorite Name(s) for this Room?
- ☐ Powder Room
- ☐ Crapper
- ☐ John
- ☐ The office
- ☐ Can
- ☐ Other....

During Your Visit Did you...
- ☐ Play with your smartphone?
- ☐ Mess with your hair?
- ☐ Inspect your teeth for food?
- ☐ Check out your butt in the mirror?
- ☐ Check your zipper/fly?
- ☐ Read through this entire guest book?

Please Tick All That Apply
- ☐ I take restroom selfies
- ☐ I snoop in medicine cabinets
- ☐ I text/call while on the toilet
- ☐ I pick my nose in the restroom
- ☐ I talk to myself while on the toilet

Doodles & Brilliant Thoughts Inspired by the Throne

Welcome to our Restroom
Please Seat Yourself!

Name: _____
Visiting From: _____
Date: _____ Time: _____
Reason for Visit: _____

Your Favorite Name(s) for this Room?
- ☐ Powder Room
- ☐ Crapper
- ☐ John
- ☐ The office
- ☐ Can
- ☐ Other....

During Your Visit Did you...
- ☐ Play with your smartphone?
- ☐ Mess with your hair?
- ☐ Inspect your teeth for food?
- ☐ Check out your butt in the mirror?
- ☐ Check your zipper/fly?
- ☐ Read through this entire guest book?

Please Tick All That Apply
- ☐ I take restroom selfies
- ☐ I snoop in medicine cabinets
- ☐ I text/call while on the toilet
- ☐ I pick my nose in the restroom
- ☐ I talk to myself while on the toilet

Doodles & Brilliant Thoughts Inspired by the Throne

Welcome to our Restroom
Please Seat Yourself!

Name: _____
Visiting From: _____
Date: _____ Time: _____
Reason for Visit: _____

Your Favorite Name(s) for this Room?
- ☐ Powder Room
- ☐ Crapper
- ☐ John
- ☐ The office
- ☐ Can
- ☐ Other....

During Your Visit Did you...
- ☐ Play with your smartphone?
- ☐ Mess with your hair?
- ☐ Inspect your teeth for food?
- ☐ Check out your butt in the mirror?
- ☐ Check your zipper/fly?
- ☐ Read through this entire guest book?

Please Tick All That Apply
- ☐ I take restroom selfies
- ☐ I snoop in medicine cabinets
- ☐ I text/call while on the toilet
- ☐ I pick my nose in the restroom
- ☐ I talk to myself while on the toilet

Doodles & Brilliant Thoughts Inspired by the Throne

 # Welcome to our Restroom
Please Seat Yourself!

Name: _____
Visiting From: _____
Date: _____ Time: _____
Reason for Visit: _____

Your Favorite Name(s) for this Room?
- ☐ Powder Room
- ☐ The office
- ☐ Crapper
- ☐ Can
- ☐ John
- ☐ Other....

During Your Visit Did you...
- ☐ Play with your smartphone?
- ☐ Mess with your hair?
- ☐ Inspect your teeth for food?
- ☐ Check out your butt in the mirror?
- ☐ Check your zipper/fly?
- ☐ Read through this entire guest book?

Please Tick All That Apply
- ☐ I take restroom selfies
- ☐ I snoop in medicine cabinets
- ☐ I text/call while on the toilet
- ☐ I pick my nose in the restroom
- ☐ I talk to myself while on the toilet

Doodles & Brilliant Thoughts Inspired by the Throne

Welcome to our Restroom
Please Seat Yourself!

Name: _____
Visiting From: _____
Date: _____ Time: _____
Reason for Visit: _____

Your Favorite Name(s) for this Room?
- ☐ Powder Room
- ☐ Crapper
- ☐ John
- ☐ The office
- ☐ Can
- ☐ Other....

During Your Visit Did you...
- ☐ Play with your smartphone?
- ☐ Mess with your hair?
- ☐ Inspect your teeth for food?
- ☐ Check out your butt in the mirror?
- ☐ Check your zipper/fly?
- ☐ Read through this entire guest book?

Please Tick All That Apply
- ☐ I take restroom selfies
- ☐ I snoop in medicine cabinets
- ☐ I text/call while on the toilet
- ☐ I pick my nose in the restroom
- ☐ I talk to myself while on the toilet

Doodles & Brilliant Thoughts Inspired by the Throne

Welcome to our Restroom
Please Seat Yourself!

Name: _____
Visiting From: _____
Date: _____ Time: _____
Reason for Visit: _____

Your Favorite Name(s) for this Room?
- ☐ Powder Room
- ☐ Crapper
- ☐ John
- ☐ The office
- ☐ Can
- ☐ Other....

During Your Visit Did you...
- ☐ Play with your smartphone?
- ☐ Mess with your hair?
- ☐ Inspect your teeth for food?
- ☐ Check out your butt in the mirror?
- ☐ Check your zipper/fly?
- ☐ Read through this entire guest book?

Please Tick All That Apply
- ☐ I take restroom selfies
- ☐ I snoop in medicine cabinets
- ☐ I text/call while on the toilet
- ☐ I pick my nose in the restroom
- ☐ I talk to myself while on the toilet

Doodles & Brilliant Thoughts Inspired by the Throne

 # Welcome to our Restroom
Please Seat Yourself!

Name: _____
Visiting From: _____
Date: _____ Time: _____
Reason for Visit: _____

Your Favorite Name(s) for this Room?
- ☐ Powder Room
- ☐ Crapper
- ☐ John
- ☐ The office
- ☐ Can
- ☐ Other....

During Your Visit Did you...
- ☐ Play with your smartphone?
- ☐ Mess with your hair?
- ☐ Inspect your teeth for food?
- ☐ Check out your butt in the mirror?
- ☐ Check your zipper/fly?
- ☐ Read through this entire guest book?

Please Tick All That Apply
- ☐ I take restroom selfies
- ☐ I snoop in medicine cabinets
- ☐ I text/call while on the toilet
- ☐ I pick my nose in the restroom
- ☐ I talk to myself while on the toilet

Doodles & Brilliant Thoughts Inspired by the Throne

 # Welcome to our Restroom
Please Seat Yourself!

Name: _____
Visiting From: _____
Date: _____ Time: _____
Reason for Visit: _____

Your Favorite Name(s) for this Room?
- ☐ Powder Room
- ☐ Crapper
- ☐ John
- ☐ The office
- ☐ Can
- ☐ Other....

During Your Visit Did you...
- ☐ Play with your smartphone?
- ☐ Mess with your hair?
- ☐ Inspect your teeth for food?
- ☐ Check out your butt in the mirror?
- ☐ Check your zipper/fly?
- ☐ Read through this entire guest book?

Please Tick All That Apply
- ☐ I take restroom selfies
- ☐ I snoop in medicine cabinets
- ☐ I text/call while on the toilet
- ☐ I pick my nose in the restroom
- ☐ I talk to myself while on the toilet

Doodles & Brilliant Thoughts Inspired by the Throne

Welcome to our Restroom
Please Seat Yourself!

Name: _____
Visiting From: _____
Date: _____ Time: _____
Reason for Visit: _____

Your Favorite Name(s) for this Room?
- ☐ Powder Room
- ☐ Crapper
- ☐ John
- ☐ The office
- ☐ Can
- ☐ Other....

During Your Visit Did you...
- ☐ Play with your smartphone?
- ☐ Mess with your hair?
- ☐ Inspect your teeth for food?
- ☐ Check out your butt in the mirror?
- ☐ Check your zipper/fly?
- ☐ Read through this entire guest book?

Please Tick All That Apply
- ☐ I take restroom selfies
- ☐ I snoop in medicine cabinets
- ☐ I text/call while on the toilet
- ☐ I pick my nose in the restroom
- ☐ I talk to myself while on the toilet

Doodles & Brilliant Thoughts Inspired by the Throne

 # Welcome to our Restroom
Please Seat Yourself!

Name: _____
Visiting From: _____
Date: _____ Time: _____
Reason for Visit: _____

Your Favorite Name(s) for this Room?
- ☐ Powder Room
- ☐ Crapper
- ☐ John
- ☐ The office
- ☐ Can
- ☐ Other....

During Your Visit Did you...
- ☐ Play with your smartphone?
- ☐ Mess with your hair?
- ☐ Inspect your teeth for food?
- ☐ Check out your butt in the mirror?
- ☐ Check your zipper/fly?
- ☐ Read through this entire guest book?

Please Tick All That Apply
- ☐ I take restroom selfies
- ☐ I snoop in medicine cabinets
- ☐ I text/call while on the toilet
- ☐ I pick my nose in the restroom
- ☐ I talk to myself while on the toilet

Doodles & Brilliant Thoughts Inspired by the Throne

Welcome to our Restroom
Please Seat Yourself!

Name: _____
Visiting From: _____
Date: _____ Time: _____
Reason for Visit: _____

Your Favorite Name(s) for this Room?
- ☐ Powder Room
- ☐ Crapper
- ☐ John
- ☐ The office
- ☐ Can
- ☐ Other....

During Your Visit Did you...
- ☐ Play with your smartphone?
- ☐ Mess with your hair?
- ☐ Inspect your teeth for food?
- ☐ Check out your butt in the mirror?
- ☐ Check your zipper/fly?
- ☐ Read through this entire guest book?

Please Tick All That Apply
- ☐ I take restroom selfies
- ☐ I snoop in medicine cabinets
- ☐ I text/call while on the toilet
- ☐ I pick my nose in the restroom
- ☐ I talk to myself while on the toilet

Doodles & Brilliant Thoughts Inspired by the Throne

Welcome to our Restroom
Please Seat Yourself!

Name: _____
Visiting From: _____
Date: _____ Time: _____
Reason for Visit: _____

Your Favorite Name(s) for this Room?
- ☐ Powder Room
- ☐ Crapper
- ☐ John
- ☐ The office
- ☐ Can
- ☐ Other....

During Your Visit Did you...
- ☐ Play with your smartphone?
- ☐ Mess with your hair?
- ☐ Inspect your teeth for food?
- ☐ Check out your butt in the mirror?
- ☐ Check your zipper/fly?
- ☐ Read through this entire guest book?

Please Tick All That Apply
- ☐ I take restroom selfies
- ☐ I snoop in medicine cabinets
- ☐ I text/call while on the toilet
- ☐ I pick my nose in the restroom
- ☐ I talk to myself while on the toilet

Doodles & Brilliant Thoughts Inspired by the Throne

Welcome to our Restroom
Please Seat Yourself!

Name: _____
Visiting From: _____
Date: _____ Time: _____
Reason for Visit: _____

Your Favorite Name(s) for this Room?
- ☐ Powder Room
- ☐ Crapper
- ☐ John
- ☐ The office
- ☐ Can
- ☐ Other....

During Your Visit Did you...
- ☐ Play with your smartphone?
- ☐ Mess with your hair?
- ☐ Inspect your teeth for food?
- ☐ Check out your butt in the mirror?
- ☐ Check your zipper/fly?
- ☐ Read through this entire guest book?

Please Tick All That Apply
- ☐ I take restroom selfies
- ☐ I snoop in medicine cabinets
- ☐ I text/call while on the toilet
- ☐ I pick my nose in the restroom
- ☐ I talk to myself while on the toilet

Doodles & Brilliant Thoughts Inspired by the Throne

Welcome to our Restroom
Please Seat Yourself!

Name: _____
Visiting From: _____
Date: _____ Time: _____
Reason for Visit: _____

Your Favorite Name(s) for this Room?
- ☐ Powder Room
- ☐ Crapper
- ☐ John
- ☐ The office
- ☐ Can
- ☐ Other....

During Your Visit Did you...
- ☐ Play with your smartphone?
- ☐ Mess with your hair?
- ☐ Inspect your teeth for food?
- ☐ Check out your butt in the mirror?
- ☐ Check your zipper/fly?
- ☐ Read through this entire guest book?

Please Tick All That Apply
- ☐ I take restroom selfies
- ☐ I snoop in medicine cabinets
- ☐ I text/call while on the toilet
- ☐ I pick my nose in the restroom
- ☐ I talk to myself while on the toilet

Doodles & Brilliant Thoughts Inspired by the Throne

Welcome to our Restroom
Please Seat Yourself!

Name: _____
Visiting From: _____
Date: _____ Time: _____
Reason for Visit: _____

Your Favorite Name(s) for this Room?
- ☐ Powder Room
- ☐ Crapper
- ☐ John
- ☐ The office
- ☐ Can
- ☐ Other....

During Your Visit Did you...
- ☐ Play with your smartphone?
- ☐ Mess with your hair?
- ☐ Inspect your teeth for food?
- ☐ Check out your butt in the mirror?
- ☐ Check your zipper/fly?
- ☐ Read through this entire guest book?

Please Tick All That Apply
- ☐ I take restroom selfies
- ☐ I snoop in medicine cabinets
- ☐ I text/call while on the toilet
- ☐ I pick my nose in the restroom
- ☐ I talk to myself while on the toilet

Doodles & Brilliant Thoughts Inspired by the Throne

 # Welcome to our Restroom
Please Seat Yourself!

Name: _____
Visiting From: _____
Date: _____ Time: _____
Reason for Visit: _____

Your Favorite Name(s) for this Room?
- ☐ Powder Room
- ☐ The office
- ☐ Crapper
- ☐ Can
- ☐ John
- ☐ Other....

During Your Visit Did you...
- ☐ Play with your smartphone?
- ☐ Mess with your hair?
- ☐ Inspect your teeth for food?
- ☐ Check out your butt in the mirror?
- ☐ Check your zipper/fly?
- ☐ Read through this entire guest book?

Please Tick All That Apply
- ☐ I take restroom selfies
- ☐ I snoop in medicine cabinets
- ☐ I text/call while on the toilet
- ☐ I pick my nose in the restroom
- ☐ I talk to myself while on the toilet

Doodles & Brilliant Thoughts Inspired by the Throne

Welcome to our Restroom
Please Seat Yourself!

Name: _____
Visiting From: _____
Date: _____ Time: _____
Reason for Visit: _____

Your Favorite Name(s) for this Room?
- ☐ Powder Room
- ☐ Crapper
- ☐ John
- ☐ The office
- ☐ Can
- ☐ Other....

During Your Visit Did you...
- ☐ Play with your smartphone?
- ☐ Mess with your hair?
- ☐ Inspect your teeth for food?
- ☐ Check out your butt in the mirror?
- ☐ Check your zipper/fly?
- ☐ Read through this entire guest book?

Please Tick All That Apply
- ☐ I take restroom selfies
- ☐ I snoop in medicine cabinets
- ☐ I text/call while on the toilet
- ☐ I pick my nose in the restroom
- ☐ I talk to myself while on the toilet

Doodles & Brilliant Thoughts Inspired by the Throne

Welcome to our Restroom
Please Seat Yourself!

Name: _____
Visiting From: _____
Date: _____ Time: _____
Reason for Visit: _____

Your Favorite Name(s) for this Room?
- ☐ Powder Room
- ☐ Crapper
- ☐ John
- ☐ The office
- ☐ Can
- ☐ Other....

During Your Visit Did you...
- ☐ Play with your smartphone?
- ☐ Mess with your hair?
- ☐ Inspect your teeth for food?
- ☐ Check out your butt in the mirror?
- ☐ Check your zipper/fly?
- ☐ Read through this entire guest book?

Please Tick All That Apply
- ☐ I take restroom selfies
- ☐ I snoop in medicine cabinets
- ☐ I text/call while on the toilet
- ☐ I pick my nose in the restroom
- ☐ I talk to myself while on the toilet

Doodles & Brilliant Thoughts Inspired by the Throne

 # Welcome to our Restroom
Please Seat Yourself!

Name: _____
Visiting From: _____
Date: _____ Time: _____
Reason for Visit: _____

Your Favorite Name(s) for this Room?
- ☐ Powder Room
- ☐ Crapper
- ☐ John
- ☐ The office
- ☐ Can
- ☐ Other....

During Your Visit Did you...
- ☐ Play with your smartphone?
- ☐ Mess with your hair?
- ☐ Inspect your teeth for food?
- ☐ Check out your butt in the mirror?
- ☐ Check your zipper/fly?
- ☐ Read through this entire guest book?

Please Tick All That Apply
- ☐ I take restroom selfies
- ☐ I snoop in medicine cabinets
- ☐ I text/call while on the toilet
- ☐ I pick my nose in the restroom
- ☐ I talk to myself while on the toilet

Doodles & Brilliant Thoughts Inspired by the Throne

 # Welcome to our Restroom
Please Seat Yourself!

Name: _____
Visiting From: _____
Date: _____ Time: _____
Reason for Visit: _____

Your Favorite Name(s) for this Room?
- ☐ Powder Room
- ☐ Crapper
- ☐ John
- ☐ The office
- ☐ Can
- ☐ Other....

During Your Visit Did you...
- ☐ Play with your smartphone?
- ☐ Mess with your hair?
- ☐ Inspect your teeth for food?
- ☐ Check out your butt in the mirror?
- ☐ Check your zipper/fly?
- ☐ Read through this entire guest book?

Please Tick All That Apply
- ☐ I take restroom selfies
- ☐ I snoop in medicine cabinets
- ☐ I text/call while on the toilet
- ☐ I pick my nose in the restroom
- ☐ I talk to myself while on the toilet

Doodles & Brilliant Thoughts Inspired by the Throne

 # Welcome to our Restroom
Please Seat Yourself!

Name: _____
Visiting From: _____
Date: _____ Time: _____
Reason for Visit: _____

Your Favorite Name(s) for this Room?
- ☐ Powder Room
- ☐ Crapper
- ☐ John
- ☐ The office
- ☐ Can
- ☐ Other....

During Your Visit Did you...
- ☐ Play with your smartphone?
- ☐ Mess with your hair?
- ☐ Inspect your teeth for food?
- ☐ Check out your butt in the mirror?
- ☐ Check your zipper/fly?
- ☐ Read through this entire guest book?

Please Tick All That Apply
- ☐ I take restroom selfies
- ☐ I snoop in medicine cabinets
- ☐ I text/call while on the toilet
- ☐ I pick my nose in the restroom
- ☐ I talk to myself while on the toilet

Doodles & Brilliant Thoughts Inspired by the Throne

Welcome to our Restroom
Please Seat Yourself!

Name: _____
Visiting From: _____
Date: _____ Time: _____
Reason for Visit: _____

Your Favorite Name(s) for this Room?
- ☐ Powder Room
- ☐ Crapper
- ☐ John
- ☐ The office
- ☐ Can
- ☐ Other....

During Your Visit Did you...
- ☐ Play with your smartphone?
- ☐ Mess with your hair?
- ☐ Inspect your teeth for food?
- ☐ Check out your butt in the mirror?
- ☐ Check your zipper/fly?
- ☐ Read through this entire guest book?

Please Tick All That Apply
- ☐ I take restroom selfies
- ☐ I snoop in medicine cabinets
- ☐ I text/call while on the toilet
- ☐ I pick my nose in the restroom
- ☐ I talk to myself while on the toilet

Doodles & Brilliant Thoughts Inspired by the Throne

Welcome to our Restroom
Please Seat Yourself!

Name: _____
Visiting From: _____
Date: _____ Time: _____
Reason for Visit: _____

Your Favorite Name(s) for this Room?
- ☐ Powder Room
- ☐ Crapper
- ☐ John
- ☐ The office
- ☐ Can
- ☐ Other....

During Your Visit Did you...
- ☐ Play with your smartphone?
- ☐ Mess with your hair?
- ☐ Inspect your teeth for food?
- ☐ Check out your butt in the mirror?
- ☐ Check your zipper/fly?
- ☐ Read through this entire guest book?

Please Tick All That Apply
- ☐ I take restroom selfies
- ☐ I snoop in medicine cabinets
- ☐ I text/call while on the toilet
- ☐ I pick my nose in the restroom
- ☐ I talk to myself while on the toilet

Doodles & Brilliant Thoughts Inspired by the Throne

Welcome to our Restroom
Please Seat Yourself!

Name: _____
Visiting From: _____
Date: _____ Time: _____
Reason for Visit: _____

Your Favorite Name(s) for this Room?
- ☐ Powder Room
- ☐ Crapper
- ☐ John
- ☐ The office
- ☐ Can
- ☐ Other....

During Your Visit Did you...
- ☐ Play with your smartphone?
- ☐ Mess with your hair?
- ☐ Inspect your teeth for food?
- ☐ Check out your butt in the mirror?
- ☐ Check your zipper/fly?
- ☐ Read through this entire guest book?

Please Tick All That Apply
- ☐ I take restroom selfies
- ☐ I snoop in medicine cabinets
- ☐ I text/call while on the toilet
- ☐ I pick my nose in the restroom
- ☐ I talk to myself while on the toilet

Doodles & Brilliant Thoughts Inspired by the Throne

Welcome to our Restroom
Please Seat Yourself!

Name: _____
Visiting From: _____
Date: _____ Time: _____
Reason for Visit: _____

Your Favorite Name(s) for this Room?
- ☐ Powder Room
- ☐ Crapper
- ☐ John
- ☐ The office
- ☐ Can
- ☐ Other....

During Your Visit Did you...
- ☐ Play with your smartphone?
- ☐ Mess with your hair?
- ☐ Inspect your teeth for food?
- ☐ Check out your butt in the mirror?
- ☐ Check your zipper/fly?
- ☐ Read through this entire guest book?

Please Tick All That Apply
- ☐ I take restroom selfies
- ☐ I snoop in medicine cabinets
- ☐ I text/call while on the toilet
- ☐ I pick my nose in the restroom
- ☐ I talk to myself while on the toilet

Doodles & Brilliant Thoughts Inspired by the Throne

Welcome to our Restroom
Please Seat Yourself!

Name: _____
Visiting From: _____
Date: _____ Time: _____
Reason for Visit: _____

Your Favorite Name(s) for this Room?
- ☐ Powder Room
- ☐ Crapper
- ☐ John
- ☐ The office
- ☐ Can
- ☐ Other....

During Your Visit Did you...
- ☐ Play with your smartphone?
- ☐ Mess with your hair?
- ☐ Inspect your teeth for food?
- ☐ Check out your butt in the mirror?
- ☐ Check your zipper/fly?
- ☐ Read through this entire guest book?

Please Tick All That Apply
- ☐ I take restroom selfies
- ☐ I snoop in medicine cabinets
- ☐ I text/call while on the toilet
- ☐ I pick my nose in the restroom
- ☐ I talk to myself while on the toilet

Doodles & Brilliant Thoughts Inspired by the Throne

 # Welcome to our Restroom
Please Seat Yourself!

Name: _____
Visiting From: _____
Date: _____ Time: _____
Reason for Visit: _____

Your Favorite Name(s) for this Room?
- ☐ Powder Room
- ☐ The office
- ☐ Crapper
- ☐ Can
- ☐ John
- ☐ Other....

During Your Visit Did you...
- ☐ Play with your smartphone?
- ☐ Mess with your hair?
- ☐ Inspect your teeth for food?
- ☐ Check out your butt in the mirror?
- ☐ Check your zipper/fly?
- ☐ Read through this entire guest book?

Please Tick All That Apply
- ☐ I take restroom selfies
- ☐ I snoop in medicine cabinets
- ☐ I text/call while on the toilet
- ☐ I pick my nose in the restroom
- ☐ I talk to myself while on the toilet

Doodles & Brilliant Thoughts Inspired by the Throne

 # Welcome to our Restroom
Please Seat Yourself!

Name: _____

Visiting From: _____

Date: _____ Time: _____

Reason for Visit: _____

Your Favorite Name(s) for this Room?
- ☐ Powder Room
- ☐ Crapper
- ☐ John
- ☐ The office
- ☐ Can
- ☐ Other....

During Your Visit Did you...
- ☐ Play with your smartphone?
- ☐ Mess with your hair?
- ☐ Inspect your teeth for food?
- ☐ Check out your butt in the mirror?
- ☐ Check your zipper/fly?
- ☐ Read through this entire guest book?

Please Tick All That Apply
- ☐ I take restroom selfies
- ☐ I snoop in medicine cabinets
- ☐ I text/call while on the toilet
- ☐ I pick my nose in the restroom
- ☐ I talk to myself while on the toilet

Doodles & Brilliant Thoughts Inspired by the Throne

 # Welcome to our Restroom
Please Seat Yourself!

Name: _____
Visiting From: _____
Date: _____ Time: _____
Reason for Visit: _____

Your Favorite Name(s) for this Room?
- ☐ Powder Room
- ☐ Crapper
- ☐ John
- ☐ The office
- ☐ Can
- ☐ Other....

During Your Visit Did you...
- ☐ Play with your smartphone?
- ☐ Mess with your hair?
- ☐ Inspect your teeth for food?
- ☐ Check out your butt in the mirror?
- ☐ Check your zipper/fly?
- ☐ Read through this entire guest book?

Please Tick All That Apply
- ☐ I take restroom selfies
- ☐ I snoop in medicine cabinets
- ☐ I text/call while on the toilet
- ☐ I pick my nose in the restroom
- ☐ I talk to myself while on the toilet

Doodles & Brilliant Thoughts Inspired by the Throne

 # Welcome to our Restroom
Please Seat Yourself!

Name: _____
Visiting From: _____
Date: _____ Time: _____
Reason for Visit: _____

Your Favorite Name(s) for this Room?
- ☐ Powder Room
- ☐ Crapper
- ☐ John
- ☐ The office
- ☐ Can
- ☐ Other....

During Your Visit Did you...
- ☐ Play with your smartphone?
- ☐ Mess with your hair?
- ☐ Inspect your teeth for food?
- ☐ Check out your butt in the mirror?
- ☐ Check your zipper/fly?
- ☐ Read through this entire guest book?

Please Tick All That Apply
- ☐ I take restroom selfies
- ☐ I snoop in medicine cabinets
- ☐ I text/call while on the toilet
- ☐ I pick my nose in the restroom
- ☐ I talk to myself while on the toilet

Doodles & Brilliant Thoughts Inspired by the Throne

Welcome to our Restroom
Please Seat Yourself!

Name: _____
Visiting From: _____
Date: _____ Time: _____
Reason for Visit: _____

Your Favorite Name(s) for this Room?
- ☐ Powder Room
- ☐ Crapper
- ☐ John
- ☐ The office
- ☐ Can
- ☐ Other....

During Your Visit Did you...
- ☐ Play with your smartphone?
- ☐ Mess with your hair?
- ☐ Inspect your teeth for food?
- ☐ Check out your butt in the mirror?
- ☐ Check your zipper/fly?
- ☐ Read through this entire guest book?

Please Tick All That Apply
- ☐ I take restroom selfies
- ☐ I snoop in medicine cabinets
- ☐ I text/call while on the toilet
- ☐ I pick my nose in the restroom
- ☐ I talk to myself while on the toilet

Doodles & Brilliant Thoughts Inspired by the Throne

Welcome to our Restroom
Please Seat Yourself!

Name: _____
Visiting From: _____
Date: _____ Time: _____
Reason for Visit: _____

Your Favorite Name(s) for this Room?
- ☐ Powder Room
- ☐ Crapper
- ☐ John
- ☐ The office
- ☐ Can
- ☐ Other....

During Your Visit Did you...
- ☐ Play with your smartphone?
- ☐ Mess with your hair?
- ☐ Inspect your teeth for food?
- ☐ Check out your butt in the mirror?
- ☐ Check your zipper/fly?
- ☐ Read through this entire guest book?

Please Tick All That Apply
- ☐ I take restroom selfies
- ☐ I snoop in medicine cabinets
- ☐ I text/call while on the toilet
- ☐ I pick my nose in the restroom
- ☐ I talk to myself while on the toilet

Doodles & Brilliant Thoughts Inspired by the Throne

 # Welcome to our Restroom
Please Seat Yourself!

Name: _____
Visiting From: _____
Date: _____ Time: _____
Reason for Visit: _____

Your Favorite Name(s) for this Room?
- ☐ Powder Room
- ☐ Crapper
- ☐ John
- ☐ The office
- ☐ Can
- ☐ Other....

During Your Visit Did you...
- ☐ Play with your smartphone?
- ☐ Mess with your hair?
- ☐ Inspect your teeth for food?
- ☐ Check out your butt in the mirror?
- ☐ Check your zipper/fly?
- ☐ Read through this entire guest book?

Please Tick All That Apply
- ☐ I take restroom selfies
- ☐ I snoop in medicine cabinets
- ☐ I text/call while on the toilet
- ☐ I pick my nose in the restroom
- ☐ I talk to myself while on the toilet

Doodles & Brilliant Thoughts Inspired by the Throne

Welcome to our Restroom
Please Seat Yourself!

Name: _____
Visiting From: _____
Date: _____ Time: _____
Reason for Visit: _____

Your Favorite Name(s) for this Room?
- ☐ Powder Room
- ☐ Crapper
- ☐ John
- ☐ The office
- ☐ Can
- ☐ Other....

During Your Visit Did you...
- ☐ Play with your smartphone?
- ☐ Mess with your hair?
- ☐ Inspect your teeth for food?
- ☐ Check out your butt in the mirror?
- ☐ Check your zipper/fly?
- ☐ Read through this entire guest book?

Please Tick All That Apply
- ☐ I take restroom selfies
- ☐ I snoop in medicine cabinets
- ☐ I text/call while on the toilet
- ☐ I pick my nose in the restroom
- ☐ I talk to myself while on the toilet

Doodles & Brilliant Thoughts Inspired by the Throne

Welcome to our Restroom
Please Seat Yourself!

Name: _____
Visiting From: _____
Date: _____ Time: _____
Reason for Visit: _____

Your Favorite Name(s) for this Room?
- ☐ Powder Room
- ☐ Crapper
- ☐ John
- ☐ The office
- ☐ Can
- ☐ Other....

During Your Visit Did you...
- ☐ Play with your smartphone?
- ☐ Mess with your hair?
- ☐ Inspect your teeth for food?
- ☐ Check out your butt in the mirror?
- ☐ Check your zipper/fly?
- ☐ Read through this entire guest book?

Please Tick All That Apply
- ☐ I take restroom selfies
- ☐ I snoop in medicine cabinets
- ☐ I text/call while on the toilet
- ☐ I pick my nose in the restroom
- ☐ I talk to myself while on the toilet

Doodles & Brilliant Thoughts Inspired by the Throne

 # Welcome to our Restroom
Please Seat Yourself!

Name: _____
Visiting From: _____
Date: _____ Time: _____
Reason for Visit: _____

Your Favorite Name(s) for this Room?
- ☐ Powder Room
- ☐ Crapper
- ☐ John
- ☐ The office
- ☐ Can
- ☐ Other....

During Your Visit Did you...
- ☐ Play with your smartphone?
- ☐ Mess with your hair?
- ☐ Inspect your teeth for food?
- ☐ Check out your butt in the mirror?
- ☐ Check your zipper/fly?
- ☐ Read through this entire guest book?

Please Tick All That Apply
- ☐ I take restroom selfies
- ☐ I snoop in medicine cabinets
- ☐ I text/call while on the toilet
- ☐ I pick my nose in the restroom
- ☐ I talk to myself while on the toilet

Doodles & Brilliant Thoughts Inspired by the Throne

Welcome to our Restroom
Please Seat Yourself!

Name: _____
Visiting From: _____
Date: _____ Time: _____
Reason for Visit: _____

Your Favorite Name(s) for this Room?
- ☐ Powder Room
- ☐ Crapper
- ☐ John
- ☐ The office
- ☐ Can
- ☐ Other....

During Your Visit Did you...
- ☐ Play with your smartphone?
- ☐ Mess with your hair?
- ☐ Inspect your teeth for food?
- ☐ Check out your butt in the mirror?
- ☐ Check your zipper/fly?
- ☐ Read through this entire guest book?

Please Tick All That Apply
- ☐ I take restroom selfies
- ☐ I snoop in medicine cabinets
- ☐ I text/call while on the toilet
- ☐ I pick my nose in the restroom
- ☐ I talk to myself while on the toilet

Doodles & Brilliant Thoughts Inspired by the Throne

Welcome to our Restroom
Please Seat Yourself!

Name: _____
Visiting From: _____
Date: _____ Time: _____
Reason for Visit: _____

Your Favorite Name(s) for this Room?
- ☐ Powder Room
- ☐ Crapper
- ☐ John
- ☐ The office
- ☐ Can
- ☐ Other....

During Your Visit Did you...
- ☐ Play with your smartphone?
- ☐ Mess with your hair?
- ☐ Inspect your teeth for food?
- ☐ Check out your butt in the mirror?
- ☐ Check your zipper/fly?
- ☐ Read through this entire guest book?

Please Tick All That Apply
- ☐ I take restroom selfies
- ☐ I snoop in medicine cabinets
- ☐ I text/call while on the toilet
- ☐ I pick my nose in the restroom
- ☐ I talk to myself while on the toilet

Doodles & Brilliant Thoughts Inspired by the Throne

Welcome to our Restroom
Please Seat Yourself!

Name: _____
Visiting From: _____
Date: _____ Time: _____
Reason for Visit: _____

Your Favorite Name(s) for this Room?
- ☐ Powder Room
- ☐ The office
- ☐ Crapper
- ☐ Can
- ☐ John
- ☐ Other....

During Your Visit Did you...
- ☐ Play with your smartphone?
- ☐ Mess with your hair?
- ☐ Inspect your teeth for food?
- ☐ Check out your butt in the mirror?
- ☐ Check your zipper/fly?
- ☐ Read through this entire guest book?

Please Tick All That Apply
- ☐ I take restroom selfies
- ☐ I snoop in medicine cabinets
- ☐ I text/call while on the toilet
- ☐ I pick my nose in the restroom
- ☐ I talk to myself while on the toilet

Doodles & Brilliant Thoughts Inspired by the Throne

Welcome to our Restroom
Please Seat Yourself!

Name: _____
Visiting From: _____
Date: _____ Time: _____
Reason for Visit: _____

Your Favorite Name(s) for this Room?
- ☐ Powder Room
- ☐ Crapper
- ☐ John
- ☐ The office
- ☐ Can
- ☐ Other....

During Your Visit Did you...
- ☐ Play with your smartphone?
- ☐ Mess with your hair?
- ☐ Inspect your teeth for food?
- ☐ Check out your butt in the mirror?
- ☐ Check your zipper/fly?
- ☐ Read through this entire guest book?

Please Tick All That Apply
- ☐ I take restroom selfies
- ☐ I snoop in medicine cabinets
- ☐ I text/call while on the toilet
- ☐ I pick my nose in the restroom
- ☐ I talk to myself while on the toilet

Doodles & Brilliant Thoughts Inspired by the Throne

www.ingramcontent.com/pod-product-compliance
Lightning Source LLC
Chambersburg PA
CBHW081233080526
44587CB00022B/3926